A souvenir guide

Eyam Hall
Derbyshire

Annie Bullen

🌳 **National Trust**

The House at the Heart of Eyam

In 1671 the Wrights, wealthy Derbyshire landowners, chose Eyam, a village reeling from the ravages of plague, as the site for their new home. Today Eyam Hall, full of family possessions, tells the story of the 11 generations who have loved this beautiful house.

A small manor house, pleasingly built of the local sandstone, sits neatly in the centre of the historic Derbyshire village of Eyam. Its high walls, elaborate gates and its position, shielded from the thoroughfare by pleasant gardens, set it apart from the smaller dwellings lining the mile-long village street. But there is no grand tree-lined driveway or landscaped park that would signal an aristocratic home. Eyam Hall was built for a prosperous middle-class family whose wealth was founded on lead mining, the acquisition of property and farming.

The Wright family, who still own this house, can trace their ancestry back to the 13th century, when Robert le Wright, who possessed land and houses in nearby Great Longstone, was born. Two-hundred-and-fifty years later Robert's descendant, William Wright was well-to-do enough to buy a considerable amount of land and some dwellings in the remote village of Eyam. It seems that these purchases in the 1630s were simply part of his property portfolio as there is no record at this time of any Wrights living in the village. It was William's son, Thomas, who, just a few years after Eyam was devastated by an outbreak of bubonic plague, built the Hall that was to be his family's home and the foremost house in the village until the present day.

Left Eyam Hall sits in the centre of the historic village

Above Pages from Peter Wright's diary, dated December 1850

Fast-forward to Christmas 1850

Peter Wright, gentleman farmer, dressed in a good suit, gives an arm to each of his sisters, Dorothy and Mary, both wearing smart hats to mark the season. This elderly trio, plump and prosperous, pink-cheeked against the cold December wind, stand on the terrace outside the entrance to Eyam Hall, their home.

The pealing bells of the nearby church of St Helen, summon them to prayers on Christmas morning 1850. The brother and sisters step down to their gate to walk past the water troughs to the church, where they acknowledge friends and neighbours, and their two farm workers, George Wilshaw and the pungently-named George Garlic. Yesterday the two Georges, at a rate of two shillings each a day, had been cleaning out pigs and loading cabbages for the 50 ewes who would soon be lambing. Today, scrubbed and suited, they are to join their employers at the Hall for Christmas dinner. Supervised by housekeeper Mary Lowe, the meal is cooking on the range in the kitchen with its flagged floors and well-scrubbed table. Perhaps a couple of geese from Peter's flock are trussed in the oven, or maybe a sirloin of beef roasts fragrantly and slowly. Later other friends and relatives have been asked to take tea with Dorothy and Mary.

Peter and his two sisters were the fifth generation of Wrights to live at the family home which was built by their great-great-great-grandfather, Thomas Wright, in 1671.

The family home

Peter, Mary and Dorothy, born at Eyam Hall, lived here until their deaths in the latter half of the 19th century. None of them married. Peter ran the family farm, of about 40.5 hectares (100 acres), mainly supporting sheep but also cows, a few pigs, geese and chickens. Arable crops included oats, while vegetables such as potatoes and turnips were grown in quantity as were mangold wurzels for fodder. Mary oversaw the dairy, while Dorothy owned property in the village.

The sisters held shares and received an annual 'pension' from their older brother, John, who inherited Eyam Hall, but never lived there. These were prosperous times, enabling the women to lead a busy, sociable life in a comfortable family home. Peter's income from the farm was augmented by profits from several lead mines and rents from property.

Peter was 30 in 1811, when he first leased the Hall from brother John, a mercer in nearby Sheffield. By that time the Hall, already 140 years old, had undergone several alterations including a new kitchen, extra bedrooms and an additional staircase. The generations of Wrights who came after Peter and his sisters continued to change the accommodation to suit their needs. They chose furniture, paintings, ornaments, glass, silver, tableware, books and other household objects for their comfort and pleasure. The rooms are completely furnished with original Wright family possessions dating from the 1670s to 2013 when the present owners, Nicola and Robert Wright, moved out.

William builds a property portfolio

The new wealthy middle classes of Victorian England had comfortable lives. Peter, our gentleman farmer, and his sisters living at Eyam Hall in the mid-19th century, were no exception. They enjoyed a leisurely rural way of life made possible by the business acumen of their great-great-great-great grandfather, William Wright of nearby Great Longstone. In the early 1600s, William, head of one of the foremost families in north Derbyshire, was venturing afield to buy land and property.

Drawn to the village of Eyam, a few miles north of his family home, in 1633 he embarked on a spending spree, adding at least 30 separate pieces of land and some substantial property to his assets. Minerals and metals, including lead and coal, were abundant here. It is probable that William bought parcels of land to prospect for lead. One hundred years on, in the early 18th century, the family records show financial interests in at least 24 lead mines in and around Eyam. William also bought a large house, described in the legal language of the time as a 'Capitall Messuage'. That came with 'Houses, Outhouses, Barnes, Stables, Gardens, Orchards, Yards' listed in the indenture of 10 September 1633 which conveyed the property from Thomas Braye to William Wright.

Eyam Hall, built by William's son, Thomas, almost 40 years later, was constructed around other older buildings. It is possible that William's 1633 investment was the foundation for today's house, although this can't be verified. What is certain is that when Thomas's son, John Wright, was due to wed Elizabeth Knyveton, Eyam Hall was built as a wedding present for the young couple.

Above The Main Bedroom

Far left Children's coats hang in the downstairs corridor outside the Entrance Hall

Below The Oak Bedroom, including the beautiful crewelwork bed hanging belonging to Elizabeth Wright, 1672. When conserved her initials were found embroidered on it

Out of the shadow

John's bride, Elizabeth, daughter of a wealthy lawyer from the village of Knyveton near Ashbourne, might have had qualms about moving to a village crushed by a major outbreak of bubonic plague, only six years before her marriage.

If that were so, her reservations were unfounded. She and John moved into Eyam Hall a year or so after their wedding and there she stayed until her death in 1700.

Devastated though the village was by the disease which killed 259 of its inhabitants between 1665 and 1666, there could be no denying its wonderful setting beneath a high plateau of dark gritstone and shale. The more gentle view towards the south overlooks the 'white peak' area where limestone predominates.

If Elizabeth were to visit today she would find her way along the winding main street, running from east to west. She would recognise many of the cottages, including the three 'Plague Cottages' that lie next to her old home. She might wonder why the church, that she knew as 'St Helen's' is now dedicated to St Lawrence, and she would see that the main road into Eyam was now the steep and winding Eyam Dale rather than the little lane that she knew at Lydgate. She would wonder too at the peacefulness of the village without the mess and stench of the many small lead mines, now defunct, on which much of the Wright family's wealth was based.

Gateway to the peaks

Even though Elizabeth Wright was the lady from the Hall, owning a carriage and horses for travel of any distance, she would have walked in and around her village, for pleasure and exercise. Maybe she took her four young children, Thomas, Anne, Dorothy and Elizabeth up the steep paths that lead to Eyam Edge, a vast plateau of rocky gritstone, from where they would have gazed for miles north and south across what is now the Peak District National Park. Their view would have been obscured here and there by the thick smoke belching from smelting works that turned the ore from hundreds of small mines into lead, but the natural beauty of the rolling landscape with its rocky outcrops and green valleys could not have escaped them.

Puzzling name

The plateau above Eyam is one of many such gritstone 'edges' in the Peak District – magnets for walkers and tourists who wonder at the lack of peaks implicit in the name of the area. Scholars believe that the *Pecsaetan*, an Anglo-Saxon tribe whose name roughly translates as 'Peaklanders' inhabiting the region in the 6th century, gave their name to the area.

Local stone

'Gritstone' is a coarse sandstone with which many of the dwellings in Eyam, including the Hall, are built. Climbers call it 'God's Own Rock' as its texture enables them to scale obstacles with comparative ease.

Left The high plateaus of dark gritstone and shale hills overlooking Eyam Hall and village are characteristic of the Peak District

Home for an Heiress

The building of Eyam Hall saw the foundation of a new branch of the Wright family.

We don't know the circumstances of John and Elizabeth's engagement but, at the age of 22, handsome John Wright, well-connected and wealthy, was ready to marry. His was the leading family in the hamlet of Unthank. John's eye – or more likely that of his mother or father – fell on Elizabeth Knyveton, daughter of a wealthy lawyer of the village from which the family took its name. They were a handsome couple, their fortunes promising a comfortable life.

You can see their portraits in the Entrance Hall at Eyam, she to the left of the fireplace, a steady expression from almond-shaped brown eyes, her thoughtful pose belied by full red lips, a dimpled chin and russet curls straying from a richly embroidered gold and cream hair-covering. John, bolder of gaze, waves of shining hair to his shoulders, open-necked white silk shirt, seems a romantic figure.

Far right Portrait of John Wright in the Entrance Hall. The portrait of his wife, Elizabeth, sits to the left of the fireplace

John's inheritance

John was not the main heir. His father's first wife, Helen Hall, died in 1633, after their son, William, was born. Thomas married again, to Yorkshire-woman Anne Shiercliffe, who bore him two sons, Thomas and John, and six daughters. Thomas died in 1656 when John was eight years old. We don't know if half-brother, William, was brought up with him, but it seems that their father decided to split his assets, leaving the family home at Unthank to William, while the property, land and mines at Eyam went to John.

Thomas Wright the builder

Thomas Wright is a more sober character altogether. His portrait, also in the Entrance Hall, shows a man Puritan in dress, white-bibbed and black-suited, hair neatly confined by a dark scull cap. Family history says that he built this house as a wedding present for John and Elizabeth. Perhaps the knowledge that John was to inherit the Eyam properties dictated that the Hall would be built here, a new seat for the Wright family. Did he and John decide together that Elizabeth, accustomed to the comfort and luxury of her wealthy family's home, should have a new house befitting her status? Did Elizabeth, who was literate and numerate, have any say in the design of the Hall? What we do know is that John and Elizabeth both signed their marriage settlement on 1 November 1672. Her signature appears on an indenture of the same date assigning the new Hall at Eyam to John. Four days later, they were married at Castleton. Elizabeth's father, Henry, had died earlier that year, leaving a considerable sum to each of his daughters. Elizabeth is said to have brought the equivalent of at least one million pounds into the marriage.

Below This portrait of the Knyveton family, c.1660, hangs in the Entrance Hall

Family portrait

That Elizabeth Knyveton's antecedents were respected by the Wrights is not in doubt. The largest painting in the Entrance Hall shows her family – mother, Elizabeth (née Colombell), father, Henry and two small girls, Elizabeth herself and sister Anne, wary-eyed solemn children, dressed identically, flanking their parents.

Setting up home

Above The Entrance
Hall was the main room
of the house during the
17th century

Eyam was a village still in recovery from the impact of the plague in 1671, when a train of heavy wagons, bearing stone, timbers, panes of precious glass and other building materials and tools, rumbled along the village street to the building site near the church.

Some of the villagers who had survived the terrible outbreak of bubonic plague just six years earlier may have found employment among the growing encampment of craftsmen and labourers at work on the shell of a smaller house. They enlarged the rear, while completely altering the façade, adding much of the present entrance hall, and what are now the drawing and dining rooms. The rooms above were also built, while the extensions at the back were comprehensive enough for Eyam Hall to be described as a newly built house when it is mentioned in John and Elizabeth's marriage settlement of 1672. Eyam Hall is small manor house, conservative in its conception, built as a comfortable home for an up-and-coming middle-class family. These were settled times in England. The civil wars were over and Charles II had been on the throne for ten years. Yet Elizabeth and John's new house, built in the warm local sandstone, takes as its spirit the Elizabethan age with its plain well-proportioned façade and symmetrical gable ends.

The Entrance Hall
Today's Entrance Hall was the main room in the house in John and Elizabeth's day. They would

Team work
John and his father would have overseen dozens of workmen from the all-important stonemasons to wallers, plumbers, carpenters, plasterers, glaziers, smiths, sawyers and painters. Materials, from the sandstone to the lead, were abundant in local quarries and mines.

old-fashioned lines where family and servants ate together. The family might have had a private 'solar' or sitting room upstairs, but the Hall would have been the centre of the household where farm and estate business was conducted, servants paid and prayers said by all each morning. The elegant settles either side of the fireplace date from this time but their contents – sides of bacon hanging from cast-iron hooks as they cured within the cupboards – would have added a little piquancy to the atmosphere in this busy room.

An orphan heir

Elizabeth and John were unusually lucky that their children all survived to adulthood. The two girls, Dorothy and Anne, wed two brothers, Charles and Francis Potts. Dorothy was to play a major part in the upbringing of her nephew, the sadly named 'Orphan John' (pictured), the future heir to Eyam Hall.

have had servants – a cook and scullery maid, a manservant or two, a personal maid for Elizabeth and nurses for their four children, son Thomas and three daughters, Elizabeth, Anne and Dorothy. Outdoor servants perhaps included gardeners, estate and farm workers and grooms to look after the horses and family carriage.

The size and shape of the Entrance Hall – known simply as the Hall in the 17th century – suggests that Elizabeth ran her household on

The family tree

There is another, unseen, presence in this Entrance Hall. A large sheet of parchment shows the Wright family tree, written in a neat copperplate hand. The first entry is that of the 14th-century Robert le Wright who was granted the title of a house and lands at Longstone by Edward III in 1327. The last date shown on the framed document, displayed on the wall is 1852.

A John Wright, born exactly 100 years after Eyam Hall was built, inherited in 1805. This John William Wright, great-great grandson of John and Elizabeth and brother to farmer Peter and sisters Mary and Dorothy, became a successful cloth merchant in Sheffield, before the hall became his. He never lived here, although he visited often and spent his retirement in other houses in Eyam. It is thought that the document detailing the early family history was written by his son, another John, who became a solicitor.

The family tree prompts questions about the lives of siblings, once they left the shelter of Eyam Hall. The portraits of some who survived childhood hang elsewhere in the house. Who, for example, are the two pretty girls (pictured right) on the first flight of the main staircase? We know they were the sisters of the Hall's first owner, John Wright, but which ones? The family tree tells us that Dorothy, Rebecca, Anne and Mary were all alive in 1665, the date on the top painting. Their dates show that Mary had a twin, Sarah, who died in 1659 at the age of 17. Why are the sitters wearing the same beautiful grey dress and identical necklaces?

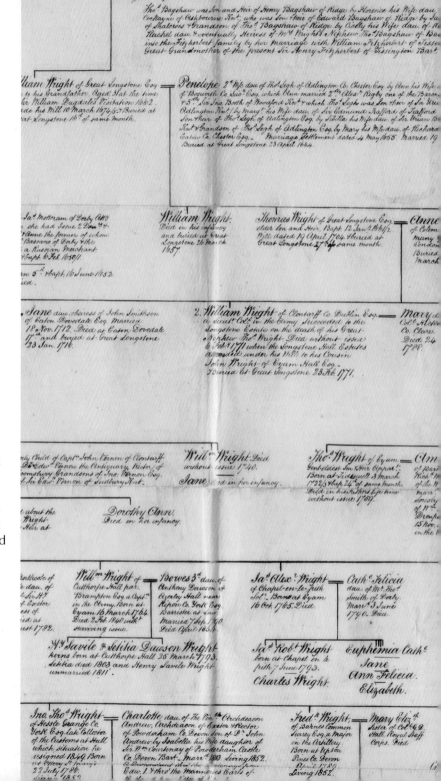

An elegant staircase

The main staircase is one of the finest features of Eyam Hall. Experts believe that it predates the 1671 house and was bought in at the time of building. It is housed in a tower that may have belonged to an earlier property on the site.

Displaying beautiful craftsmanship, it is listed by Historic England who describe it as 'an impressive early C17 dogleg staircase through three floors with turned balusters, wide moulded handrail, ball finials and pierced pendants'.

A close look shows that original windows and walls have been altered to form a new tower for these elegant steps.

Another significant portrait hangs on the landing of the backstairs. This is another John Wright – poor 'Orphan John' whose parents, Thomas and Susanna, both died in 1704, the year the lad turned four. Thomas, the only son of John and Elizabeth, inherited Eyam estate in 1693 when his father died. His mother, Elizabeth, lived at the Hall until her death in 1700. By then Thomas had married Susanna Wilkinson with whom he had four children in quick succession: John (1700), Elizabeth (born and died in 1701), Catherine (1703) and William the following year. Thomas and Susanna, the second generation to live here, had only a few years to enjoy their ownership of the house, yet, it seems, they wasted no time in making their mark and changing the domestic arrangements.

Opposite The Wright family tree is the centrepiece of the Entrance Hall

Below Crafted in the early 17th century, the elegant dogleg staircase predates the house

Orphan John Inherits

Childbirth was still a dangerous time. In 1704 young John Wright lost his mother and newborn brother. His father, Thomas, died early that year.

Thomas inherited his mother's assets in 1700 and it may have been this that prompted him and Susanna to build a new two-storey extension comprising a kitchen with a room above, at the west side of the house. They may even have built the backstairs for the use of their servants.

Times had changed and middle-class families were abandoning the old habit of using their main downstairs room for communal meals. The original kitchen stood in what is now the dining room, opening onto the Entrance Hall.

Susanna's new kitchen, with its stone floor and up-to-date iron cooking range built into one of the three arched recesses, opens onto a small rear yard with a couple of outbuildings and the washhouse containing a well, sink, fireplace and washing copper. In 1991 the fireplace wall was plastered and the alcoves turned into cupboards. Restored to its original state, it became known as the 'old kitchen'.

Susanna was just three or four months pregnant with William when her husband, Thomas, died in February 1704. It seems that she lost her own life giving birth to William, who lived just four weeks, in July of that year. So at the tender ago of four John, Susanna's first son, now an orphan, became master of Eyam Hall.

Enter the aunts

Although John and his baby sister Catherine had lost both their parents, there were plenty of aunts nearby. Thomas had three sisters, Dorothy, Anne and Elizabeth. Dorothy and Anne married two brothers, Charles and Francis Potts, the former a lawyer from Castleton. Aunt Elizabeth married an Isaac Tipping. All three families were involved in financing lead mines locally and, for some reason, had interests in Scottish mines.

Dorothy and Charles, childless at the time, looked after young John and, probably, Catherine as well. By the time John was eight and Catherine five, they had a daughter of their own, Anna, who must have become close to her cousins, brought up together in the same house. As John Wright grew into manhood he became involved in running the family estate and in the management of lead mines at Eyam and Castleton.

Anna and Archibald

One of John's business associates was Sir Archibald Grant of Moneymusk near Aberdeen. He became a Member of Parliament for Aberdeen in 1722. Heavily in debt and involved in dubious deals, he was sent to prison and lost his parliamentary seat. Somehow in 1731 he met and married Anna Potts, Dorothy's daughter and John's cousin. Anna owned a house in Castleton and some profitable mines – luckily all held in trust, so her husband couldn't get his hands on them.

Left **The Kitchen, which would have had an iron cooking range**

Above **The Larder can be found next to the Kitchen in the downstairs corridor**

Right **Commissioned by Sir Archibald Grant (standing third from right), *The Gaols Committee of the House of Commons* by William Hogarth *c.*1729 depicts the committee enquiring into the living conditions of Fleet Street's prisoners**

John and Jane

By the time cousin Anna was visiting and writing letters to her husband Archibald in Fleet Prison, Orphan John had been a happily married man for a decade. Like his grandfather he found a wealthy bride from an old-established family. To celebrate their engagement and marriage in 1721 he and Jane Farewell each had miniature portraits painted. These are displayed in the Oak Bedroom along with portraits of Jane's ancestors, paintings of a quality not seen elsewhere in the Hall.

Eclipsing them all is the *Lady in the Hat* – Jane Farewell's great-grandmother, Jane Woodward, arched eyebrows and black eyes, an ironic half-smile under that great black hat, signalling that here is a woman in control. The two men with neat beards and wary eyes are her husbands number one and two. She became Lady Farewell on marriage to her second husband, Sir John Farewell in 1641 when she was in her mid-thirties.

The Farewell ancestors were a glamorous-looking bunch although our Jane, who became Jane Wright on her marriage to John in 1721, seems altogether more down-to-earth and sensibly dressed than her forebears.

Family records show the Farewells owned land in their native Nottinghamshire, in Ireland and London. Jane's father had died when she was a child, so it is likely she brought the financial assets she had inherited to the marriage. She was a good housekeeper – she kept detailed account books and copies of some of her recipes from a tasty looking 'Italian Pudding' to 'White Quince Cakes' have been passed down through the generations.

Treasures in the Oak Bedroom

The magnificent bed in this room wasn't here in Jane and John's lifetime. It is in fact a hybrid, put together from reclaimed furniture from three different centuries. The headboard is made from a 17th-century carved chest while the 'roof' and front panel seem to be made from wall panelling from a later period. The elaborate posts may be inverted newel posts from a staircase. It once belonged to an early 20th-century family relative.

The two pieces that are likely to have been in the house (although not necessarily in this room) when John and Jane held sway, are the beautiful oak linen cupboard next to the bed and the cedar-wood coffer at its foot. When the present owners of Eyam Hall, Robert and Nicola Wright, moved here in 1990 they found today's bed coverings, dulled by age, folded into this chest, whose pungently scented wood may have preserved them from moth attack. These wonderful crewel work embroideries, showing trees, flowers, birds and animals in coloured wools, could have been part of Elizabeth Knyveton's trousseau and may even have been made by Elizabeth herself. Conservators, restoring the hangings, discovered the initials 'EW' worked into a corner.

Mystery window

The window by the bed has the name 'Jane Wright' scratched onto its surface. The panes are 18th-century glass so the Jane in question could be Jane Farewell or Jane Sisum who became her daughter-in-law in 1761.

Opposite A detail of the ornately carved bedpost and embroidered bedspread in the Oak Bedroom

Left Portraits adorn the fireplace in the Oak Bedroom, including the *Lady in the Hat* – Jane Woodward – and the miniatures painted to celebrate the marriage of John and Jane Wright in 1721

A house full of children

Despite its unpromising start, Orphan John's life was long, prosperous, fruitful and, probably, happy. The family fortunes improved further in 1771 when he inherited the Great Longstone estates from his cousin Lieut. Col. William Wright, who died childless. The two estates were now his, under one ownership for the first time.

By 1738 six sons and three daughters had been born to Jane and John at Eyam Hall. Two of the boys died in infancy but the other seven children survived.

The youngest, James Farewell, was the baby of the family. His birth and baptism along with those of his siblings, is recorded in his father's beautifully bound Baskett Bible, still in the Library. His mother Jane's prayer book, a gift from her husband in 1727, is there too.

His brother Thomas, twelve years his senior, a pillar of the community, was their father's right-hand man in business affairs and on the local magistrates' bench. This was a boom time for lead-mining in Eyam. The family had interests in more than 20 mines, including one at Cussey Grove – the location of today's visitors' car park at Eyam Hall.

The other boys, except James, joined the army. At no time could James have thought that he would own Eyam Hall, yet, through curious twists of family fate, that is what happened.

The military men

John's first son, Thomas, died in 1759, improving the inheritance prospects of brother number two, another John, an army major.

John's portrait and those of his brothers Robert and young James Farewell are displayed in the Library. John and Robert are resplendent in scarlet military tunics while James, looking boyish, well-scrubbed and solemn-faced, hair fashionably curled, is dressed probably in the livery provided with his position as Second Assistant Rider at the court of George III. It was a lowly job but enabled him, in 1761, to marry Jane Sisum, daughter of a London merchant. Jane's family were from Derby, so the pair might have been acquainted before James moved to the capital. Jane's portrait, showing a pretty, demure 18-year-old, hangs in the Library too.

James and Jane's early married life was fraught with sadness as their first four babies died in infancy. Imagine the joy when Elizabeth, born in 1767, thrived. It may not be coincidence that this was the year James was given The Firs, a family home in Eyam, by his father.

Left The Library, a room used by the whole family for both study and leisure over the years. The impressive portrait of John Wright in his scarlet military uniform hangs to the right of the bookcase

A poem
Captain Robert Wright, gazing sternly from the Library wall does not look like a romantic man. Yet it is he who is thought to have written the poem scratched onto the window, extolling the virtues of Fanny Holme of Stockport:

Fanny, ye pride of natures beauteous Powers,
Her sexes Envy, and ye Pride of Ours,
Regardless triumphs in a world of Charms,
Wins ev'ry Eye and ev'ry heart alarms.
Whenever she sings 'tis heaven to be near.
Words sweet as honey charm ye ravish'd Ear.
We stand attentive to her tuneful tongue,
As wondering Syrens when a Sapho sung.

RW

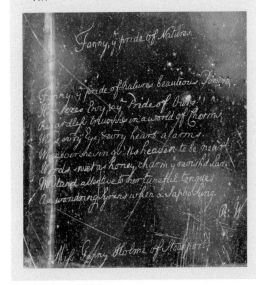

James Farewell Saves the Family Home

Sudden death and a twist in the family fortunes put Eyam Hall on the market. James stepped in at the eleventh hour to save his home.

Robert's soldiering took him away from Derbyshire to Gibraltar. He married twice – but neither time to the seductive and mysterious Fanny Holme. By 1773 his older brother John, retired from the army to a life of middle-class respectability, was living at the Hall, managing their father's affairs. John became Deputy Lord Lieutenant of Derbyshire, a Justice of the Peace and in charge of a company of local militia. His parents may have moved to Longstone Hall, leaving him in training for his future ownership of the family estates.

Robert, meanwhile, had returned to Eyam from Gibraltar sometime after his first son, John, was born in 1762. Two more sons arrived before the family moved to nearby Tideswell. They may have transferred to Longstone Hall sometime after 1771. His first wife Elizabeth was buried at Longstone in 1773.

Eventually both Longstone and Eyam became his. Brother John died in 1779 just a year before their father, leaving the way clear for Robert to inherit in March 1780.

He made Longstone his home abandoning Eyam Hall altogether. It is likely that James and Jane, now successful parents, brought up their children in the Hall. Elizabeth, born in 1761 had been joined by John William, Dorothy, Mary and Peter.

Left Portrait of James Wright in the Library, painted in the year of his marriage to Jane in 1761

Right This tiny portrait of Jane Wright, depicted here in her later years, hangs to the left of the fireplace in the Library

Just before the turn of the century the terrible news that the family home was to be sold shattered their hopes for the future. Robert, settled at Longstone, had given Eyam Hall to his son and heir, John Thomas, in 1797. The young man, now married to a wealthy woman and living in Devon, put it up for public auction. A buyer stepped forward. James Farewell Wright finally became the owner of Eyam Hall and part of its estate, saving it for his family and future generations.

A time of simple pleasures

The portraits in the Library show members of two generations who enjoyed settled lives at Eyam Hall. The Wright estates were split once more as Robert and his large family inhabited Great Longstone, while James Farewell Wright and Jane Sisum, with perhaps a sigh of relief, took ownership of the Hall, its land and the property belonging to the estate.

James and Jane, fresh-faced, are portrayed in the year of their marriage, 1761. Jane, gowned and capped, was 18, while James, in his early twenties, seems young and innocent. A tiny portrait of a very old wrinkled woman hangs to the left of the fireplace. This is Jane in old age; she lived to be 88, an achievement in those days.

Above her on the fireplace wall are three characters we've met. Peter the gentleman farmer, her last-born child and his older sisters the resolutely unmarried Dorothy and Mary with their pretty hats and candid eyes. These three lived their whole lives at the Hall as tenants of their older brother John, whose portrait occupies the fourth space. He left Eyam to become a cloth merchant in Sheffield where he lived with his wife, Alethea, and their large family.

Above Swords are displayed above the fireplace in the Entrance Hall, signifying the military carriers of the male members of the Wright family, including Robert, John and James

Clues in the Library

Eyam Hall was built with two great chambers, one atop the other. Today's Library, directly above the Entrance Hall, might have been a showy solar, or private sitting room, suitable for the refined tastes of its first lady, Elizabeth Knyveton. It was a larger room then, with other rooms opening off.

Later generations, especially Orphan John and Jane Farewell and their son and daughter-in-law James Farewell and Jane Sisum had many children. This chamber might have been partitioned to provide extra bedrooms.

Even in its diminished size the Library gives away small details of Wright family life. There are the portraits and the books – 1,042 of them, belonging to Wrights of all generations. Peter, the gentleman farmer, owned not only the practical *Every Farmer His Own Cattle-Doctor* by George Armatage, but also an edition of *New*

Grammar and collections of poems, while sisters Mary and Dorothy opted for books with surprisingly modern 'self-help' themes – a *New Week's Preparation* for Mary and Dorothy's *Essay on Happiness* by John Duncan. Their father, James Farewell Wright, who lived to be 67 owned *The Right Course of Preserving Life and Health unto Extream Old Age.*

The games they played

One of the Library's novelties is a 'pop-up' medical book. *The Anatomies of the Bodies of Man and Woman*, a rare *c.*1675 volume, shows, by means of paper flaps, anatomical detail. While the pages are in remarkably good condition, the flaps are bent – in particular the flower covering the male genitalia.

The furniture in this room, the rosewood tea table with its extending panels, the games table, inviting a chess challenge or an afternoon's

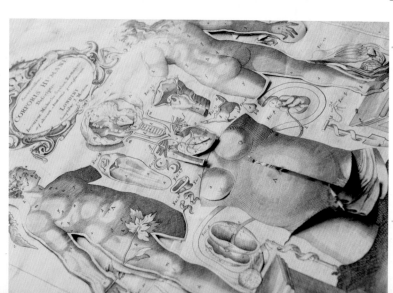

Left The 'pop-up' medical book, *The Anatomies of the Bodies of Man and Woman*, is a rare volume, *c.*1675

Right The Library at Eyam Hall gives away small details of the Wrights' family life

Opposite A detail of the rosewood games table in the Library

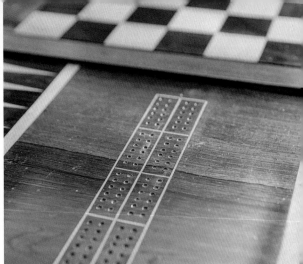

backgammon, give an idea of contented leisure hours: tea, perhaps with cakes or biscuits made from family recipes, a good gossip, an hour or so reading quietly by the south-facing windows. The lovely oak bureau with its built-in writing table and secret drawers invites use and we know that Peter Wright was a tireless letter-writer, corresponding with many friends and especially his niece Maria Rawson, his late sister's daughter. Maria, wealthy and independent, was just ten years younger than her uncle. They discussed farming, business affairs, social outings and holidays.

Peter and his sisters stayed at Eyam Hall when its owner, their older brother, John Wright the mercer retired. He moved to another family house in Eyam. Two of his unmarried daughters, Mary and Jane, also living nearby, must have spent many social hours with their two aunts and Uncle Peter at the Hall.

On John's death in 1853 he left the Hall to his son John, a lawyer, and the other half of the estate to his oldest boy, James, a surgeon. Peter and the sisters lived out their lives here until 1862 when Peter died, leaving enough money for his housekeeper, Mary Lowe, to buy a cottage. On his death his nephew John moved in with his family.

Stitches of Time

Some very fine tapestries hang in just one room. No-one knows where they are from or when they were hung.

Here is another Eyam Hall mystery. Who bought these tapestries – some very old and fine? When were they hung? Who decided to cut them to size, to cover the walls of this small room just as we would use wallpaper today? And what was this room? Too small to be a reception chamber or parlour, it has been partitioned at some time from a larger area perhaps as a sewing or sitting room.

But when was it decorated with these colourful wall-hangings? The tapestries were certainly here when Peter Wright leased the Hall from his brother, John. His tenancy agreement, written clearly in his own hand states in part: 'I agree to accept the tenancy of the Hall at the rent fixed between us – my brother & myself – (vis £40 per an; £20 of which during the first year of my occupancy is to be spent in repairs); I promise not to alter the color of the doors of the House; not to make any changes in reference to the tapestry work now hanging on the walls of the Room known as the Tapestry Room.' This agreement could have been made any time after 1805 when their father died and John inherited the estate.

A severed head and a fruity picnic

The tapestries have been made to fit the walls, thus losing the main picture in some cases. But to the right of the door are two biblical scenes which appear to show Jehu, King of Israel, being crowned with a laurel wreath and comely widow, Judith holding the gory head of the drunken Assyrian general Holofernes. She had beheaded him when he threatened to conquer her city, Bethulia.

Left A tapestry of Jehu, King of Israel, being crowned with a laurel wreath

Right This exquisite 15th-century Flemish tapestry depicts a wedding scene. Its bright colours have remained unchanged because it was originally hung the wrong way round

A happier picture emerges in the brightly coloured piece filling the corner to the right of the window. This fine work in silk and wool is Flemish, made in the 15th century. It shows a jolly gathering of well-dressed men and women in a sylvan setting, enjoying each other's company and passing around a large plate filled with fruit, including strawberries. This is the finest piece in the room and the brightest. By design or happy accident it was originally hung the wrong way round, thus preserving the colours which are now on show in a controlled setting.

Conservation work

When Robert and Nicola Wright inherited Eyam Hall in 1990, the tapestries were the worse for wear, damaged by soot, smoke and sunlight. They were clumsily tacked to wooden battens and in obvious need of restoration. After cleaning and mending they were hung, using velcro, onto a treated timber frame. Filters on the windows prevent damage from ultra-violet light.

The Professional Generations

Law, medicine and the church claimed the next generations as income from the land and mining dwindled.

Peter Wright, gentleman farmer, deeply involved in village affairs and living comfortably with his sisters at Eyam Hall, must have wondered what the future held when his elder brother, John, died in 1853. John, the Hall's owner, retired from his cloth business in Sheffield, had been living in another family home in Eyam.

The Wrights at the time owned The Firs, a substantial house, near Hawkhill Road, and the Brick House, across the road from the Hall. A census puts John at The Firs after his retirement, but it is likely he used both houses at different times. Peter, Dorothy and Mary, now in their seventies

Above Photographs of John Wright and his daughters on the mantelpiece in the Library

and eighties, had made the Hall their own. Peter ran his farming enterprise with the help of the two Georges, Wilshaw and Garlic, while overseeing his mining and property investments and charitable work. His sisters kept house, entertained their friends and looked after the kitchen garden and the dairy which helped augment the family income.

Peter's notebooks

Peter, like many Wrights who lived here, was not the owner. His notebooks detail the pounds, shillings and pence of daily life from paying Robert White for 'making a Ring and putting it in the Bull's Nose' to settling with his sister £5/9/0 for a suit of clothes. Theirs was a busy domestic life. He was a Commissioner in the Property and Income Tax Court and Captain in the South High Peak Battalion of Volunteer Infantry (a sort of 'Dad's Army' to counter the threat from Napoleon). He was generous with gifts to friends who needed help and to the church and village school. His cows were all given names such as 'Flora' and 'Swindel', while he called his bull 'Lupin' and rejoiced when healthy calves were born.

Top right Inside the pollard oak writing cabinet in the Library

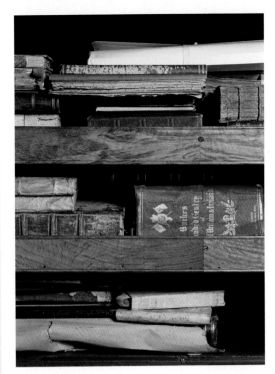

John and Peter must have discussed the future. John left the Hall and part of the estate to his younger son, also John, a solicitor. The other half of the estate went to his firstborn, James Farewell Wright, a surgeon, living and working in Sheffield.

Peter, Dorothy and Mary need not have worried. Their nephew, John, the lawyer, waited until first the sisters and then Peter, who died in 1862, were buried in Eyam churchyard before he and his family moved into the Hall. There is a small photograph of John on the Library mantelpiece as well as those of his daughters, Harriet and Margaret, who steered the fortunes of the Hall through the end of the century, the end of the Victorian and Edwardian eras and to the first years of the First World War, when Harriet died and left the family home to her cousin William Peter Wright, a vicar. William had already inherited the other half of the estate from his father, Charles Sisum Wright, also a man of the cloth, and son of James the surgeon.

The Women of Eyam Hall

Since the Hall was built in 1671, its women have been educated, literate and very often in charge of their own financial affairs.

We've said goodbye to Peter, good citizen, farmer and master of Eyam Hall, but what of the hidden lives of his sisters, Dorothy and Mary, spinsters, first encountered with him on that Christmas morning in 1850?

They died, each 86; Dorothy in 1858, Mary two years later. 'Spinsters' is what they would have been called during their funerals in Eyam church. However, Dorothy and Mary, women of means, chose to stay at the centre of the household, free to enjoy friends and family without facing the perils of childbirth or the prospect of submission to a husband's authority. They owned shares and property and had control over their lives.

They were born into a large household which included their father's unmarried sister, Aunt Dorothy, who probably taught them their letters and numbers, housekeeping skills and the management of a kitchen garden and orchard. Their great-great-grandmother, Elizabeth Knyveton, for whom Eyam Hall was built in 1671, was a wealthy and lettered woman, bringing a fortune to her marriage with John Wright. She

Right Portrait of Maria Rawson, displayed in an alcove in the Dining Room

ensured her marriage settlement had 'right of dower' (the right to stay on in the marital home after her husband's death) and she was able to leave property and investments to her daughters, son and grandson. It is understood that she was the sole executrix of her father's will – remarkable for a woman in those days.

Maria Rawson

One of the most interesting Wright women was Maria Rawson, another niece of Dorothy and Mary. Maria, whose portrait is in the Dining Room, was born to their older sister Elizabeth Wright in 1791. Elizabeth, married to James Rawson, died two years later.

The Rawsons, her father's wealthy family, were from Sheffield where Maria later owned her own property, Glenview House. But she had roots in Eyam too and here we must resurrect Peter Wright, her uncle and particular friend. Peter, ten years older than his niece became her confidant and business associate. Maria visited Eyam often, where she owned land and property. In 1859 she paid for a clock to be fitted into the tower of Eyam church and she left money to help local widows and single elderly women. She and Peter wrote regularly to each other, organising outings and discussing farming matters.

'Dear Maria, Thank you for your letter this morning. I have got one also from Mrs Peacock; I will write to her and say she may expect us to tea on Thursday ... I quite agree with you about the half past one train; we will be in time and bring Miss Carrington', wrote Peter in September 1852. The rest of the letter implies Mrs Peacock runs a guest house at Scarborough and that they are to stay there.

Left The clock face on Eyam church, paid to be fitted into the tower by Maria Rawson in 1859

Above Hairbrushes on the dressing table in the Oak Bedroom, decorated with the initials EJW, belonging to Elizabeth Wright

The War Years

Increasingly those who inherited Eyam Hall lived elsewhere. But it was rarely unoccupied, the family still regarding the old house as the most reliable of homes.

When Peter Wright died in 1862, his nephew John, the Hall's owner, moved in with his wife, Mary and their daughters, Margaret and Harriet. By 1883 both John and Mary had died.

The girls occupied the house, with a dwindling number of servants, until first Margaret died in 1906 and Harriet, who looked after their portion of the estate and researched family history, in 1915. The Hall now belonged to Harriet's cousin William, whose mother, Charlotte, owned the rest of the Eyam estate.

In June 1917, a tea party took place at Eyam Hall. Mother and daughter Charlotte and Emily Wright, having moved in a couple of months earlier, invited the rest of the family to tea in the garden of their new home. Charlotte's grand-

Below The Dining Room

Right Off to war in 1914. Charles is second left on the front row

daughter, Dorothy Wright, then an energetic young woman of 22, kept a diary before and during the war. She notes that after the party 'most of us walked back to Sheffield, arriving nearly at midnight'.

It is likely that Dorothy's father, William, and her mother, Winnie, were at the celebration. William, vicar of the church of St Silas, Sheffield, about 12 miles from Eyam, now owned the Hall, while his mother, Charlotte, inherited the rest of the Eyam estate, when William's father, Charles Sisum Wright, died in 1903. William, then a grown man, might have been embarrassed by his portrait (now in the Dining Room) showing a bright-faced nine-year-old boy, hair neatly combed, wearing the uniform of his new school, Repton, near Derby.

William and Winnie

A photograph of William as a young man shows he inherited his mother's deep-set intelligent eyes and resolute jaw. Her portrait as a young woman, dark-haired, steady of gaze, hangs in the Dining Room. William and his own wife, another Charlotte, known as 'Winnie', met when both fathers were priests in charge of Doncaster parishes.

Times had changed and the adventurous young couple, married in 1891, travelled to Europe that October, the first of many trips to the continent and, later, North Africa and Canada. They returned, with a box full of photographs, to live with William's family at Stokesley rectory in Yorkshire where William was curate to his father. They moved to Hemingbrough, North Yorkshire, with their children, Charles Sisum and Dorothy, and then to Sheffield just before cousin Harriet died at Eyam.

Dorothy's diaries tell us they left Hemingbrough vicarage in April 1915 'after spending 10 happy years under its roof'. She notes the day in early July that year when her father visited cousin Harriet 'who was very ill' at Eyam. Harriet died a few days later, leaving William in possession of the Hall.

Above Photograph of Charlotte Winifred, otherwise known as 'Winnie', with her son Charles and daughter Dorothy

Dorothy's diaries

On the day war was declared, 4 August 1914, Dorothy, on holiday from her boarding school at Eastbourne, played in a tennis tournament with her older brother, Charlie, at Cliffe, in Yorkshire. Their grandmother, Charlotte, lived in the village. Charles, an undergraduate at Trinity College, Oxford, resolved to join up. Dorothy records a few weeks later, on Sunday 12 September, 'Charlie left by 10.25 for London to Selby to join the School Special Corp camp on Upson Downs. All drove to see him off.'

By Christmas Charlie, a 2nd Lieutenant in the Territorial Force was away from home.

'The most wretched Xmas day I remember,' mourned Dorothy, 'missed Charlie dreadfully.' She cheered up the following May, when Charlie, stationed at Northampton, telephoned home: 'a marvellous invention the telephone! Could hear him speak quite distinctly'.

She was spending more time at Eyam, helping prepare the Hall for its new incumbents, 'Grandmama and Auntie' who 'removed' there on 25 April 1917. 'Elsie and I went to Eyam for day by 8.05 train and came back with Dad in evening on Walsh's removing van.' On 11 July, Charlie, now a Captain, embarked for France. 'Dad, Mother and I went with Charlie to see him off to Southampton from Waterloo at 11.55, bound he knew not where – What a ghastly war! He went in the best of spirits with two friends.' A week later: 'Dad, Auntie, Constance, Ivy and I biked to Haddon. Ate lunch in the Hall field and went on to Bakewell and back by Baslow – lovely ride. Biked 21 miles.'

Left A young Charles Wright in his army uniform, c.1914

Top right A panorama of the Battle of Ypres, October 1914. Charles was stationed here in 1918 until the end of the war

Right A photograph of the Battle of Ypres in 1918, where Charles fought until returning safely home later that year

Horrid news and a ceasefire

Imagine Dorothy's dismay when the family discovered in October that Charles had been injured and hospitalised – before being passed fit to go back to the Front near Ypres. But all ended well when Charles arrived safely home later in the year and, eventually, Dorothy was able to write on 11 November 1918: 'Armistice signed with Germany; Fighting ceased at 11am; Thrilling day.'

By now Dorothy's grandmother, Charlotte, and Aunt Emily were well settled in at Eyam Hall where Dorothy visited, pushing 'Grandmama' out in her bath chair along the country lanes. Charlotte died in the autumn of 1919 and, at last, the entire Eyam estate returned to one owner: Dorothy's father, William.

William, still a parish priest in Sheffield, was not ready to retire just yet and it seems that Eyam Hall became a holiday and summer home for the family, although Aunt Emily, who never married, may have stayed on there when she wasn't travelling in Europe. Charles returned to Trinity College, Oxford to complete his studies and decide what course his life should take.

The family comes home

William and Winnie waited until his retirement in 1923 to move into Eyam Hall, with their diary-keeping daughter, Dorothy. At some point William's sister, Emily, moved into nearby Brick House, where she died in 1925.

The last family celebration of William's priesthood was the marriage of his son, Charles Sisum, to his childhood sweetheart, Irene Yeoman. The wedding took place in 1922 at St Peter's church, Stokesley, where Charles's grandfather, after whom he was named, had been Rector and Rural Dean, and where William had served his curacy.

In August 1919 Charles, showing more pragmatism than romance, had written a letter to the 22-year-old Irene: 'I am writing to assure you of my real love for you. Should you accept it, I cannot promise when we should be married, perhaps not for 18 months or even 2 years, should your mother and father give their consent. I think we know each other well enough to justify the decision I have come to because we have never been real strangers!' He confides he is deciding between the Civil Service, the church or perhaps 'school mastering' and wouldn't ask

Right Childhood sweethearts Charles and Irene whose happy marriage lasted more than 60 years; their portraits can be seen in the Dining Room

Opposite Photograph of Charles and Irene's wedding day in the Dining Room

(From left to right) Irene's brother, Dorothy Wright, William Peter, Charlotte Winifred, Charles, Irene, Irene's father (Dr Yeoman), Irene's mother, an unknown man, an unknown lady and an unknown bridesmaid

her to marry until his career was settled. Irene, showing some surprise, didn't quite turn him down: 'Charlie, I think I am hardly ready to be engaged yet, but perhaps in a few months time … When you come we can talk things over, it is so much easier than writing.'

Charles and Irene, whose happy marriage lasted more than 60 years, until his death in 1985, moved to the Hall in 1946 when he had retired from 'school mastering', his chosen career. Their portraits are in the Dining Room. Charles, pictured later in life, grey-haired, fine-featured, carries a look of authority, arising perhaps from those years teaching French and History at King Edward VII school, Sheffield, where he was fondly known as 'Daddy Wright'. Irene, a sweet-faced young woman, later threw herself into village life.

Middle-aged by the time they moved to the Hall, they knew there would be no children. But, despite the war, they found themselves, the owners of the 'big house', at the centre of Eyam's considerable charitable and social activity.

A benevolent couple

Charles' parents, William and Winnie had enjoyed their retirement, travelling around the world, but also becoming involved in village affairs – he bell-ringing, she becoming an expert needlewoman. Even today villagers remember their grandparents telling them that William, the only car-owner in Eyam, was in demand for lifts to hospital when babies were on their way. Winnie died in 1937 and her husband in 1944, during the war. Both are buried at Eyam.

A Blessing or a Curse?

Gone were the days of servants to help run a large house. Those who inherited beautiful old homes in the 20th century had to be prepared for the inevitable costs of repairs and maintenance.

A mixture of emotions must have confounded Charles and Irene as they planned their move. Irene was leaving a comfortable house in Broomhill, Sheffield, and a fulfilling social life. Charles enjoyed singing with many musical organisations and choirs and took part in amateur theatricals. Whatever her apprehensions Irene took up her new life with energy and enthusiasm. Beautiful and imposing, the house had large rooms, draughty corridors and leaded windows through which the wind whistled.

Below The Drawing Room, where Irene would sit each day

But they fell into village life. Charles became Secretary of the Eyam Tennis Club and a school governor. He involved himself with local planning matters, sang in the church choir and trod the boards with the Parish Church Players. Irene founded a Women's Institute group, becoming President. She hosted a sewing circle and opened the gardens for the church fête and many other fundraising events.

A successor

Charles and Irene, childless, knew that their successor was to be Robert Wright, born in 1948, two years after they moved to Eyam. Robert, brought up at Longstone, is a descendant of Captain Robert Wright, whose son, John Thomas Wright on marrying an heiress from Devon, moved to that county, selling Eyam Hall to his cousin, James Farewell Wright, in 1797.

Robert was told when he was 12 that Eyam Hall would eventually be his and he spent much of his childhood visiting Charles and Irene,

delighting in racing up and down the staircases, exploring the attics, cellars and gardens. As he grew older he realised that this inheritance would be a mixed blessing. The estate had dwindled to 100 hectares (250 acres), many of the houses and cottages sold off and the dozen or so that remained were in need of expensive repairs and renovations – as was the Hall itself and the buildings in the stableyard.

Robert, a lawyer, and his wife Nicola, a speech therapist, moved with their young family to Eyam to help Charles and Irene manage the Hall. They lived in The Firs, a family house that has seen many generations of Wrights come and go. Charles and Irene gradually confined themselves to a few rooms in the house: the Dining Room, the Kitchen and the Drawing Room, where Irene would sit each day in the shadow of a massive ceiling beam. When Robert and Nicola moved to the Hall in 1990, they discovered that beam to be dangerously unsafe. The older couple celebrated their 60th wedding anniversary at the Hall in 1982. Charles died at home three years later. He was 91. Irene, by now living and sleeping in the Dining Room and looked after by helpers and carers, followed him in 1990, at the age of 93. Nicola and Robert, the new owners, were facing the biggest decision of their lives.

Left Photograph of a young Charles Wright, who later became Secretary of Eyam Tennis Club

Above Charles and Irene in old age outside the front door of Eyam Hall

The family business

Eyam Hall, the height of luxury in 1672, was, by the end of the 20th century, no longer a comfortable family home. The gardens had become overgrown, while rooms that had fallen out of use were filled with broken furniture and pictures crying out for restoration. Robert and Nicola, the 11th generation of the Wright family to inherit the Hall, had to decide whether to make it their home. In 1990 they and their three young children moved in.

Nicola threw herself into a major clear-up. She and Robert set up living quarters for themselves and the children, earmarking rooms and objects for restoration. Family portraits, the tapestries, and some pieces of furniture underwent expert cleaning and mending. The old kitchen, unsuitable for family use with its plastered-over walls, quarry-tiled floor and badly-adapted 17th-century table was next on the list and the Aga was moved to another room earmarked for

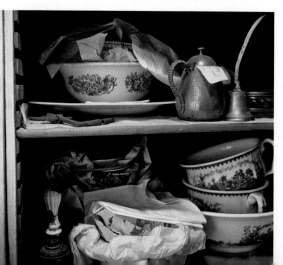

family use. The appliance removed, Nicola and Robert uncovered three deep recesses underneath stone arches and original flagstones hidden beneath the tiles, revealing the room built for Thomas and Susannah Wright in 1700.

Opening the house

Nicola and Robert knew that if they were to keep the Hall they would have to open it to the public. Not long after they had moved in, a young woman who had completed a heritage interpretation course, knocked on their door asking if they wanted her help. Caroline Fooks offered her services for a few months, and was still involved six years later, allowing Nicola to complete a Master's Degree in Tourism Hospitality.

Above When Nicola and Robert took on Eyam Hall in 1990, they found many of the paintings abandoned and in need of restoration

Left A cupboard full of fine chinaware and crockery was tagged for restoration in the big clear-up by Nicola and Robert Wright in 1990

The Nursery

Toys and dolls belonging to many generations of Wright children have been brought together in the Nursery. This room, once the cook's bedroom, houses a rocking horse bought for Charles and Dorothy Wright in the 1890s and dolls belong to Irene Yeoman, who married Charles in 1922. The large doll, named 'Catherine' and the green teddy bear belonged to Gwen Cockrem, a niece of William Peter's wife, Winnie. The 1850s Georgian-style doll's house may have belonged to Harriet and Margaret Wright who moved here in 1862.

On 29 March 1992 the late Duchess of Devonshire cut the ribbon and the first visitors arrived, eager to see this house, full of the furniture, possessions and lives of one family who kept their home for more than 300 years. But there was much more to be done. Estate cottages had to be updated and maintained and the stable block to the side of the Hall renovated with the addition of a Craft Centre, a café and shop.

The Wrights were forward-thinking, exploring all options for the Hall. They offered weddings. Nicola planned courses for local schoolchildren about life in a house before the days of electricity, running water and central heating. For more than 20 years the couple committed themselves to the restoration of the Hall, estate buildings and stable courtyard.

Letting go

Twenty years later, once their three children, Jeremy, Felicity and Timothy, had grown up and moved away, Robert and Nicola decided it was time to retire. But, as other generations of Wrights had discovered, Eyam Hall is not a house that lets go easily.

Nicola and Robert both felt they had grown to know the family characters whose portraits are displayed on the walls. They had an opinion about each one – not always complimentary. It was not hard to imagine, as they moved from room to room, that they shared the house with the ancestors: Peter writing at his desk in the Library, Dorothy and Mary sewing in the Tapestry Room. Tempting smells of food cooking on the Old Kitchen fire, while children and dogs of generations long-gone filled the hall with noise as visitors came and went.

Both understood very well that visitors who had explored Eyam Hall under their stewardship had been able to identify with the house because of its manageable size and the nature of its contents – nothing too grand or pretentious but bits and pieces collected over 300 years to add to the family's comfort and enjoyment of their home.

The Trust takes over

Nicola and Robert's dilemma was real and pressing. The Hall still had to pay its way if it was to stay in the family, but they no longer felt able to manage the day-to-day running of the business, nor did they want to be the first Wrights for almost 350 years to walk away from the house. Their children were not in a position to take over. Help came from an unexpected quarter.

The National Trust agreed to the stewardship of Eyam Hall, under a lease. Although the history of the house is domestic and the contents homely, they tell the story of one family over more than 300 years. From the 17th century, the Wrights enjoyed the same lives as hundreds of other aspirational middle-class families of those times.

It is precisely the stories of these hidden lives, in a house small enough to feel lived-in yet old and unchanged enough to conjure the past, that attract interest.

Eyam Hall, re-opened under the care of the National Trust in the spring of 2013, is still owned by the Wright family. Robert and Nicola, who moved into another house in the village, continue to maintain the fabric of the building.

Community involvement
Robert and Nicola Wright continue to find time to play a full part in village life. Robert was involved with the church music while Nicola directs local plays and pantos, and has been school governor and parish councillor. Both are volunteers at the village school.

Opposite A young visitor in the Dining Room

Left A family exploring inside the manor house

The Stable Courtyard and Gardens

The history of the outbuildings and gardens is still being uncovered. The large garden, divided into four sections, is both pretty and productive.

On 21 September 1850, Peter Wright noted that one of his two farm-hands, George Garlic, was hard at work in the garden, earthing celery. For the rest of that month and into the next George was digging and clearing beds and borders. Peter and his sisters would certainly have insisted that their garden was not only flower-filled, but also used to grow food for the house.

What we know of the history of the walled garden is sketchy, but for much of its life it would have been productive, with a glasshouse for fruit and well-manured beds growing vegetables for the house. Certainly when the Hall was built in 1671, its first mistress, Elizabeth Knyveton, would have ensured that herbs for culinary and medicinal use were grown, while salads and vegetables were brought into the Kitchen on a daily basis. It is likely that several hives full of bees stood here to pollinate the apples, plums and

Left View through the archway to the back door in the walled garden

These outdoor rooms were first fashionable in Elizabethan times when guests left the dinner table indoors to enjoy sweetmeats and fruit in a more intimate setting.

The stable courtyard, a centre of activity in the days when the farm was linked to the Hall, would have housed a dairy, probably a brewhouse and possibly a slaughterhouse, stables and a carriage house. Now the old buildings are occupied by a café, craft workers selling their goods, local produce shops, the National Trust offices and shop.

Research is underway to discover more about the garden whose stone walls, steps and terraces and stone paths are all Grade II listed, as are the buildings in the Stable Courtyard.

pears and to provide honey for the kitchen and wax for the hundreds of candles necessary for the household. A small flock of sheep, kept for their wool and meat, grazed the orchards, providing natural manure for the fruit trees.

In the 17th-century households such as Eyam Hall were self-sufficient in many of the basics of life, from beer and ale to cheese, butter and bread, probably from wheat grown on the home farm. Chickens would be kept for their eggs and meat. The walled garden today is divided into four sections. Espaliered apples are grown on the sunny walls, while lawned areas are brightened by flower borders. A stone 'banqueting house' – a two-storied structure whose upper room is reached by a flight of stone steps – stands against the garden wall.

Above The stable courtyard today, home to a café, the National Trust offices and craft shops

Right The greenhouse in the walled garden. Peter Wright and his sisters would insist the garden was both decorative and productive

The Village

Eyam is one of many villages in the exceptionally beautiful Peak District. Its fame is built on the heroic sacrifice made during the dreadful 1665–6 plague outbreak.

The village of Eyam winds at length below the dark gritstone hills to the north and above the lighter limestone landscape to the south. To the east flows the River Derwent. One clue to the Anglo-Saxon origin of Eyam is its name, which derives from the Anglo-Saxon 'Aiune', meaning 'place by the water'.

The main village street curves its way almost a mile between cottages and houses built of the local stone, many of them 200 or 300 years old. Along the way there are clues to an industrious past and a thriving present. In the 18th century silk was woven in several premises. One hundred years later at least seven small factories produced shoes in Eyam. The tannery at nearby Grindleford which made high-quality leather meant that Eyam and nearby villages became centres of cottage industries, often with whole families working to produce the leather goods.

Above Water Lane winds into the heart of Eyam village

Right Stone troughs can be found all around the village, once supplying fresh water to the residents of Eyam

Clues to the past

At the Townhead end of the village is Hawkhill Road where Eyam Museum tells the tragic story of the outbreak of bubonic plague (see pages 48–55) that struck the village in 1665. Other exhibits explain the silk-weaving and shoe-making businesses, while a fossil and mineral collection gives an insight into the geology of the area.

The village green still plays host to the stocks, where justice was meted out to miscreants. In the days when dozens of lead mines were dotted in and around Eyam the beleaguered occupant of this primitive but effective punishment device was generally a lead miner deemed to have flouted his rights. The building at the back of the green was once the 'market hall' where farmers would sell their produce.

Behind the museum lie the ruins of Bradshaw Hall, once the grandest house in Eyam but fallen into decay a decade before the Wrights began to build in 1671. Towards the end of the 16th century the Bradshaw in residence, Col. Francis Bradshaw, designed what might have been the first public water supply in the country. As you walk through the village today you'll notice series of stone troughs, the water flowing from one to the other. These are the originals, using water piped from the plentiful springs that rise in the village.

Eyam poets

Set back from the street is Olde House, the birthplace of Eyam's poet, Richard Furniss. An early romantic poet and novelist, Anna Seward (pictured), was born in the rectory, next to the church, in 1742. Major John Wright, a stout bachelor, retired from the army and living at Eyam Hall, is said to have fallen violently, if briefly, in love with her.

The village today

Eyam Church is dedicated to St Lawrence, although for most of its history it was named for St Helen, the mother of Constantine the Great. The name was changed in the early 20th century. Some authorities date the earliest part of the building to the first half of the 12th century, but it is agreed that the nave was built in about 1350. The paintings in the nave, whitewashed over in 1643 during the Civil War, were uncovered and conserved more than 300 years later in 1963. Some had been destroyed earlier when the chancel arch was built in 1868.

Of the six bells, four are ancient, dating from the decades before the plague, but two, cast in 1926 were hung in memory of the Wright family. Tablets in the vestry also bear the memory of the Wright family, while their burial vault is found in the churchyard. Between the church and the Hall is the site of the famous Eyam sheep roast when a whole sheep is roasted on a spit to celebrate the Carnival. It's an old tradition. Visitors still flood into the village to taste the local delicacy of oat cakes baked in mutton fat.

Left The Wright family symbol on the family burial vault in Eyam churchyard

Above Eyam church, dedicated to St Lawrence

Wakes Week and well dressing

The traditional festival of Wakes Week is celebrated at the end of August, starting on a Saturday with the age-old blessing of the wells at Town Head and Town End. The wells are 'dressed' for the occasion with elaborate decorations, where a mosaic picture is composed by arranging flower petals, berries, seeds, moss, lichen, fruit skins, feathers, leaves, cones or anything else natural into a frame of puddled clay pressed into heavy wooden boards. The annual Plague Commemoration service happens the following day, before a week of events, competitions and entertainment, is rounded off with the Carnival on the final Saturday.

The imposing building opposite the church is the Mechanics' Institute, founded in the mid-19th century as an adult educational centre aimed at working men. Now it is the meeting place for every village organisation and social group. It hosts classes, pantos, shows and fundraising events.

The Square, a pleasant open area, was once home to the cruel practice of bull-baiting – you can still see the ring where the unfortunate creature was tethered. Today it's more peaceful with small shops and a tea room and the reputedly haunted Miner's Arms, now the only pub in a village once noted for its numerous hostelries.

The Miner's Arms

The Miner's Arms, opened in 1630 as The King's Head, underwent its name change when it became the venue for the Barmote Court, dealing with mining disputes and rights in the area. The Eyam and Stoney Middleton Association for the Prosecution of Felons – an organisation founded in 1812 by Peter Wright amongst others and of which Robert Wright is a current member – still meets here.

Right The festival spirit comes to Eyam village every year during Wakes Week

The Plague

On the gate of the village primary school, just along the road from the church, is inscribed a familiar children's song:

Ring-a-ring o' roses,
A pocket full of posies,
A-tishoo! A-tishoo!
We all fall down ...

That this refers directly to the bubonic plague, the dreaded 'Black Death' which swept through Britain in waves from 1347 onwards, is uncertain – but the words describe the progress of the disease with deadly accuracy (see panel).

Death came suddenly to Eyam in early September 1665. The weather had been exceptionally hot and the village was settling into its usual routines after the excitement of Wakes Week at the end of August.

Left Verses from the familiar children's song, which refers directly to the plague, are inscribed on the gates of the village primary school

Above The Plague Cottages, where the disease that devastated the village in 1665 began

In one of the cottages lying between Eyam Hall and the church lived Mary Hadfield, the newly remarried widow of a prosperous yeoman, Edward Cooper, who had died in 1664, leaving money and land. The executor of his will was his 'beloved and trusty friend', Thomas Wright of Unthank, the landowner who would build Eyam Hall a few years hence. Mary had two young sons, Jonathan and Edward Cooper. Her new partner, Alexander Hadfield, a travelling tailor, was away, leaving his business in the hands of his assistant George Viccars, who lived with the family.

The fatal package

When a carrier knocked at the cottage door with a large and heavy bundle, wrapped in some sort of rough cloth, George Viccars took it inside and eagerly shook it open. It is likely that the parcel contained not only new material but also second-hand clothing that he planned to use as patterns for new suits and dresses to be worn by his customers in Eyam. He was dismayed that the material, rolled up tightly, felt damp. It had been ordered some time ago, and had been brought by carrier all the way from London – where the plague was rife.

There was a good fire in the cottage and George, shaking out the bolts of material propped it on the drying racks where it steamed gently as the moisture escaped. He probably noticed one or two fleas hopping away and he might have scratched as he was bitten. Fleas were a fact of life in 17th-century villages. Within a week George Viccars was dead. No-one connected the now-abandoned cloth with his terrible demise. The fleas in the cloth had been carrying the plague *bacillus* from the infected rats on whose blood they had fed in London.

Death from the plague
The 'rosy ring' is the rash that was often the first indication of infection together with a strange sweet smell that filled the nostrils of the victim. The 'posies' could refer to this or to the nosegays carried to ward off the disease. Sneezing, the precursor of the fatal fever, was followed by 'falling down' – or dying.

Fear as the disease spreads

The sudden, unexplained death of a man who was not native to the village might have been forgotten after a few days. But by the end of September, three weeks after Viccar's burial, five others in neighbouring cottages had died, including little Edward Cooper, Mary Hadfield's younger son. By now the villagers knew their enemy. Fear spread through Eyam prompting a few to flee. But most had nowhere to go and who would welcome a refugee from a village where plague was rife?

Twenty-nine died in seven weeks. As October ended more had been killed by the plague than had perished each year for the last decade. The villagers' only hope was that the cold of approaching winter would kill the disease. But by now the fleas had jumped from humans to the rats living in barns and cottage rafters. This food source kept the plague alive as 1665 slipped away and the new year was seen in without any joy. At April's end, 73 men, women and children had been buried and with that toll came the dread that rising temperatures would mean more losses. But May saw only two deaths from the plague and hopes, faint at first, began to rise.

Hope proved premature. The death rate soared in June. Something had to be done.

Direction came from the church. Two men, one old, the other in his twenties, one a staunch Puritan, the other a Church of England rector, formed a plan for dealing with the terrible disease. William Mompesson and Thomas Stanley put aside their differences to keep their community together.

Heroic sacrifices

Mompesson, Eyam's newly-appointed rector, and Stanley, a previous incumbent, much loved in the village, had little in common except their desire to help the villagers. Stanley, a Dissenter, had resigned his living when he could not accept the Act of Uniformity and the new Book of Common Prayer.

Both men called a meeting to put their plan to the villagers. Firstly, there would be no funerals or churchyard burials, freeing the clergymen and Mompesson's wife, Catherine, to look after the sick and dying and to help prepare wills. Villagers were asked to bury their own dead in fields or gardens. Secondly, they agreed that the church would be shut and open air services held to prevent infection. A natural amphitheatre, Cucklett Delph, not far from the church, was the chosen spot, where Mompesson could preach from a high rock. The third agreement was to quarantine the village, imposing a *cordon sanitaire* to prevent the spread of the disease. It was this decision that put the remote Derbyshire village into the pages of history books and made it famous for nobility and sacrifice in the face of death.

Shallow graves
Burials had to be swift to prevent infection. Bodies were dragged, using a sheet, or rope to hastily dug, shallow graves, often marked with a stone decorated with a home-made cross chiselled onto its surface.

Opposite Engraving of Elizabeth Hancock. She had the heart-breaking task of burying her husband and six children in eight days

Below This painting of the Riley Graves by John Platts is now displayed in Eyam Museum

The dreadful toll

The self-imposed boundary was drawn as the death rate rose steadily. Inhabitants of this close-knit community, grimly waiting for the next victim to fall, held to their pledge to remain within the village.

Measures were put in place to ensure that those who lived would be fed.

Free food and medicines, promised and paid for by the Earl of Devonshire at Chatsworth, were left at the southern edge of the village. Other dropping-off points for paid-for goods were the now-called 'Mompesson's Well' about a mile out of the village and several spots in the hills to the north. If there was running water, coins were left in the flow to ensure they were infection free. Money left at the Boundary Stone, off Mill Lane, was placed in vinegar-filled holes.

Mompesson, Stanley and Catherine Mompesson spent their days visiting the sick,

Below The Riley Graves, burial site of the Hancock family

Tragedy beyond telling

The statistics tell little of the depth of the individual human tragedies suffered daily. Among the first to die were John Syddall and four of his children. They had lived near the tailor's cottage. A surviving daughter, Emmott, betrothed to Rowland Torre from nearby Stoney Middleton, saw her lover secretly throughout the winter. She missed their assignation in April, but loyal Rowland, hearing of the 'quarantine' held to his faith that she lived. Imagine his despair when, the village safe once more, he rushed to her house to find it deserted. His sweetheart had died late in April.

One man who recovered from the infection and prospered from the plague was lead miner Marshall Howe, whose cottage can be seen at Townhead, in Tideswell Lane. Howe, believing himself immune, appointed himself parish sexton, offering to dig graves and bury the dead. His fee was the appropriation of goods and chattels in the house of the victim. His ruthlessness came at a cost; his wife and son died, perhaps from infected goods brought into the house.

comforting families and writing wills. The Mompessons' two young children had been sent away to relatives but Catherine, not strong, succumbed to the disease at the end of August 1666, the month when almost 80 died. Catherine is the only known plague victim buried in the churchyard. Each 'Plague Sunday' at the end of August, red flowers are placed on her tomb by the current vicar's wife.

The shape of the village has changed little since 1665. Today's visitors can walk to the Boundary Stone, Mompesson's Well and Cucklett Delph. The terrible toll on some families is detailed outside the cottages they occupied. The Riley Graves, a short walk away, are the resting places of seven members of the Hancock family, all buried by the wife and mother, the only one of them to survive.

Top left Mompesson's Well, another site where paid-for goods were dropped off for the quarantined villagers of Eyam

Left Holes in the Boundary Stone, where coins are still left in honour of the plague victims and their sacrifice

A village in shock

By November 1666 it was all over. Christmas approached but there was little emotion left for celebration. Two-hundred-and-fifty-nine villagers out of about 800 lay buried in graves in gardens, fields and hillsides. Those who had left at the beginning returned to find homes derelict, animals roaming the streets, fields and gardens overgrown. Relatives and friends in neighbouring villages were wary about resuming contact.

In 1670 the village lost the two men who had guided them through the terrible months of the plague. William Mompesson, for months exhausted and depressed by the death of his beloved Catherine, remarried and moved with his new wife, Elizabeth Newby, to the parish of Eakring, in Nottinghamshire. Thomas Stanley, whose strong principles and unwavering Puritanism had not lost him the affection of the villagers, died that year. There is a memorial tablet to him in the churchyard although the whereabouts of his grave is unknown.

The tipsy rector

There is a strange postscript to these tragic events concerning a tipsy rector, a hasty marriage and a vengeful jilted fiancée. The tale of the Rev Joseph Hunt, appointed rector of Eyam in 1683, is an extraordinary story, with an important historical consequence. Having to conduct a baptism in the Miner's Arms, the young parson drank rather more than he could handle, flirted outrageously with the landlord's daughter, Anne Fearns, and found himself 'married' to her when a guest, using Joseph's own prayer book, joined their hands and read the Marriage Service.

The scandalous 'wedding' reached the ears of the Bishop who insisted it was binding and must be repeated – in church this time.

Unfortunately for Joseph and Anne, the young man was already engaged to a wealthy woman who sued him for breach of promise, sending the bailiffs to arrest him. They fled into the church for sanctuary and it seems they spent the whole of their married lives there, living in a lean-to 'room' where they raised several children.

Because Joseph dared not leave the church, he undertook the lengthy task of compiling a bound register of the parish records, hitherto on separate parchment sheets. These included each of the plague deaths, now neatly written down and recorded in one place. Anne died in 1703 and Joseph six years later. Even their burial took place inside the church because the bailiffs would have been allowed to exhume their bodies from the graveyard and expose them to some macabre 'punishment'.

Left Pathway through Eyam churchyard

What Lies Ahead?

Eyam Hall, a 17th-century gem, has been the home at the centre of village affairs for centuries. Now it is looked after by the National Trust.

Eyam Hall, built in the shadow of the terrible events of 1665 and 1666, signalled a turn of the tide in the affairs of the village. The Wrights were wealthy businessmen, owning profitable mines and land, much of it in Eyam. The Hall, with its estate and farmland, brought employment and prestige. Its construction was a vote of confidence in a village struggling back onto its feet. From its completion in 1672 the Hall has been at the heart of Eyam. The 18th and 19th centuries favoured middle-class enterprise and the Wrights prospered.

They were not grand. They had no titles nor were they involved in affairs of state or court. Their duties lay at home, in the county where they served as magistrates and in the village as presidents of organisations, employers and caretakers of the land.

But the Industrial Revolution and two world wars changed their lives. Small manor houses became costly burdens, beautiful, but hard to maintain without an expensive workforce to look after the housekeeping, the gardens and the fabric of the building.

Inheritance can be a mixed blessing. Each generation of Wrights has clung to the family home. For a few years at least it is in the care of the National Trust but still owned by Robert and Nicola Wright, whose much-loved family home it was for more than 20 years.

Above The back door in the walled garden at Eyam Hall, leading to the church in the distance